A Grammar of the Sgaw Karen

A GRAMMAR

OF THE

SGAW KAREN

By Rev. DAVID GILMORE, M. A.,

*Of the American Baptist Mission
in Burma.*

RANGOON:

AMERICAN BAPTIST MISSION PRESS,

F. D. PHINNEY SUPT.

1898.

FIRST EDITION, 1898.

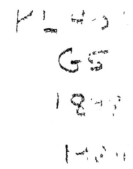

PREFACE.

This book has been called forth by the needs of the American Baptist Karen Mission in Burma. For many years there has been in print no book from which a beginner could learn the grammatical principles of the Karen language. Dr. Mason's Anglo-Karen grammar has long been out of print; and even when a copy could be secured, it was (owing to the incomplete state in which it was left) very perplexing to a neophyte, though very valuable to the more advanced student. Dr. Wade's *Karen Vernacular Grammar* does not begin to be of much assistance until the student is able to read Karen, although the English remarks interspersed throughout it may be used at an earlier period.

The book here offered students of Karen does not pretend to be an exhaustive grammar of the language. The author's aim has been to introduce beginners to the principles of Karen grammar. He has not attempted to account for every idiom of the Karen language; still less has he aimed to do the work of a lexicographer.

The author acknowledges heavy indebtedness to the works of Dr. Mason and Dr. Wade. He has drawn upon these sources with less scruple as they are not generally available to beginners in Karen. His thanks are due to the Rev J. N Cushing, D. D., and the Rev. D. A. W. Smith, D. D., for encouragement and assistance in the inception of the work, and to the Rev. W. F. Thomas, M A., for a critical reading of the manuscript.

DAVID GILMORE.

A GRAMMAR OF THE SGAW KAREN.

INTRODUCTION.

1. The Karen language, in its grammar, presents striking analogies to the English. Like the English, it depends mainly on the order of words for expressing its syntactical relations, and the order of words is much the same as in English.

2. The Karen differs from the English in being a monosyllabic language. Its words, with some real and some apparent exceptions, are monosyllables. The accidents of case, gender, person, number, time, etc., are expressed, some (as the person of the pronouns and the gender of certain nouns) by the intrinsic signification of the words, some (as the case of nouns) by the position of the words in the sentence, and some (as the accidents of verbs) by certain particles prefixed or affixed to the root.

3. The two grand principles of Karen grammar are enunciated with substantial correctness, though not with perfect accuracy, by Dr. Wade: "1st, Any root or combination of roots, becomes a noun, pronoun, adjective, verb, adverb, preposition or conjunction, according to the office it performs in a sentence. 2nd, Each syllable, or root, has a signification of its own, and a grammatical relation to one or more of the other syllables in every compound part of speech."

THE ALPHABET.

4. The Karen Alphabet is derived from the Burmese. It consists of 25 consonants and 10 vowels, with 6 tones, the character သ appearing among both consonants and vowels.

THE CONSONANTS

5. The consonants, with their names and powers, are as follows—

က	ကးဒိၣ်ထံး	*k*
ခ	ခးကစီၤ	*kh*
ဂ	ဂ့ၢ်ကျၢၢ်လီၤ	*gh*
ဃ	ဃးဒိၣ်	*ch*
င	ငးဒ့ၣ်ချၢ	*ng*
စ	စးတဖျၢၣ်	*s*
ဆ	ဆးတဘံ	*hs*
ၡ	ၡးခွဲၢ်	*sh*
ည	ညးညိၣ်နီၣ်	*ny*
တ	တးဝၢ်ရ	*t*
ထ	ထးတဃံၣ်	*ht*
ဒ	ဒးတဒါ	*d*
န	နးတဆံး	*n*
ပ	ပးတဒိ	*p*
ဖ	ဖးပဝံၣ်	*hp*
ဘ	ဘးတကူး	*b*
မ	မးခွံးသး	*m*
ယ	ယးဘီထိ	*y*
ရ	ရးကွၣ်	*r*
လ	လးကွၣ်ကိၣ်	*l*
ဝ	ဝးကစီၤ	*w*
သ	သးဒိၣ်ဃီၤ	*th*
ဟ	ဟးကွၣ်လီၤ	*h*
အ	အးခံဆီ	—
ၢ	ၢၤကတၢၢ်	*hh*

6 The powers assigned to the consonants in the above table do not in all cases perfectly represent the sounds of the Kare [illegible] Th [illegible] may assist the learner i [illegible] represented

exactly in English, though his main reliance must be upon the living teacher

ကက has a sound intermediate between *k* and *g*.

ခ is the aspirate of ကက. It is pronounced like *kh* as heard in the phrase *brick house*, or in *Bokhara*.

ဂ has no analogue in the European languages.

ဃ is pronounced like *ch* in the German *bach*, or the Scottish *loch*.

င is pronounced like *ng* in *sing*, or *n* in *ink*.

စ has a sound intermediate between *s* and *z*.

ဆ is the aspirate of စ. It has the sound of *ssh*, as heard in the phrase *hiss him*.

ဈ is pronounced like *sh* in *shun*.

ည is pronounced like *ñ* in *cañon*, or *ny* in *lanyard*.

ဋ has a sound intermediate between *t* and *d*.

ဌ is the aspirate of ဋ. It is pronounced like *th* as heard in the phrase *hot house*.

ပ has a sound intermediate between *p* and *b*.

ဖ is the aspirate of ပ It is pronounced like *ph* as heard in the phrase *hap hazard*.

သ is pronounced like *th* as heard in *thin*.

အ as a consonant has no sound of its own; it is a mere stem to which vowel signs are attached.

ဠ has no analogue in the European languages.

When any one of these consonants stands alone it is pronounced with the sound of the short vowel *a*, as in *quota*.

If the learner will remember to breathe hard in pronouncing the aspirates ခ, ဆ, ဌ and ဖ, he can hardly fail of getting the correct sound.

DOUBLE CONSONANTS.

7. When one consonant follows another with no vowel sound intervening, the second consonant is represented by a

symbol, which is joined to the character representing the first consonant. The consonants capable of such combination, with their symbols, and illustrations of their combination with the consonant ဘ, will be found below.

ဂ	ၢ	ဘၢ	*bgh*
ယ	ျ	ဘျ	*by*
ရ	ြ	ဘြ	*br*
လ	ၠ	ဘၠ	*bl*
ဝ	ွ	ဘွ	*bw*

VOWELS.

8 As has already been said, every consonant, when written alone, is understood to be followed by the short sound of *a*, as heard in *quota*.

9. This sound, when standing alone, is represented by the character အ.

10. Other vowel sounds are represented by symbols joined to the consonants which they follow.

11. When such vowel sounds stand alone, their symbols are joined to the character အ.

12. The vowel symbols alone, and in combination with အ and ဘ, are shown below.

	အ	*a*	ဘ	*ba*
ါ	အါ	*a*	ဘ	*ba.*
ံ	အံ	*i*	ဘံ	*bi*
ၢ	အၢ	*o*	ဘၢ	*bo*
ု	အု	*u*	ဘု	*bu*
ူ	အူ	*u*	ဘူ	*bu*
့	အ့	*e*	ဘ့	*be*
ဲ	အဲ	*è*	ဘဲ	*bè*
ိ	အိ	*o*	ဘိ	*bo*
ၣ	အၣ	*aw*	ဘၣ	*baw*

13. The subjoined table explains more definitely the powers of the vowels.

- အ, *a* in *quota*.
- အါ, *a* in *father*.
- အိ, *i* in *machine*.
- အၢ, German *o* in *Gothe*, or *u* in *Turkey*.
- အု, German *u* in *Gluck*, French *u* in *lune*.
- အူ, *u* in *rule*, *oo* in *moon*.
- အေ, approximately *a* in *rate*.
- အဲ, French *è* in *Molière*, or *e* in *met*.
- အီ, *o* in *note*.
- အံ, *aw* in *raw*.

TONES.

14. In Sgaw Karen, every syllable consists of a vowel, either alone, or preceded by a single or double consonant. A syllable always ends in a vowel. Every syllable may be pronounced in six different tones of voice, the meaning varying according to the tone in which it is pronounced.

15. Where no tone is marked, the syllable is pronounced with a rising inflection

A syllable marked with ၢ် (အၢသံ) is pronounced with a heavy falling inflection.

A syllable marked with ာ် (အးသံ) is pronounced abruptly, at a low pitch.

A syllable marked with း (ဖျၢၣ်သံး) is pronounced abruptly at an ordinary pitch.

A syllable marked with ၣ် (ဟးသံ) is pronounced with a falling circumflex inflection.

A syllable marked with ၤ (ကူၣ်ဒိ) is pronounced with a prolonged even tone.

16. When the above mentioned signs follow ါ, the ါ is omitted for the sake of brevity; *e. g.*, instead of ကါၢ် we write ကၢ်.

SUPERNUMERARY CHARACTERS.

17. A few characters not belonging to the Sgaw Karen alphabet have been introduced, and are occasionally used in transliteration from English into Karen.

The Burmese ခ (pronounced ?) is sometimes used to represent the English *j* or soft *g*.

The Pwo Karen inflection ၂ (ကၠၟၜၩ:) is sometimes used to represent a final *l* in an English syllable. It is pronounced like ၣ.

ARBITRARY CHARACTERS.

18. ၣ is generally pronounced like ခ:, and ၥ like ၐၩ; but at Tavoy and Mergui they are sometimes pronounced like ၕၩ and ၐၩ respectively.

PUNCTUATION.

19. English punctuation marks are used. The comma, period and quotation marks are commonly used, the exclamation point and semicolon less commonly, the colon and the interrogation point not at all.

FIGURES

20. The Numerals are as follows—

0	1	2	3	4	5	6	7	8	9
၀	၁	၂	၃	၄	၅	၆	၇	၈	၉

The Arabic system of notation is used

THE STRUCTURE OF THE SENTENCE.

21. The order of words in Karen may be illustrated by the following simple sentence: ၐၩၯၬၯၬၑၩ, *Saw Wa builds a house.* ၐၩၯၬ, *Saw Wa,* subject; ၯၬၑ, *builds,* predicate; ၯၬၑ, *house,* object; ၯၩ, a particle used to mark the close of a declarative sentence.

A Karen ~~sentence~~ ~~therefore~~ ~~resembles~~ ~~an~~ English sentence in t··· ﹐ ﹐ ··· —

(1) The order of words is: subject, predicate, object.

(2) The subject and object are recognized by their position in the sentence.

22. Modifiers may be added to the above sentence as follows: တ ဘၣ်ဘၣ်စီၤဝါ သးပှၢ်နၣ်သူၣ်ထီၣ်ဟံၣ်ချ့ချ့ဘိၤ, *Sometimes old Saw Wa builds a house quickly.* တ ဘၣ်ဘၣ်, *sometimes*, adverbial modifier; သးပှၢ်, *old*, adjective modifying စီၤဝါ; နၣ်, demonstrative adjective modifying စီၤဝါ; ချ့ချ့, *quickly*, adverb modifying သူၣ်ထီၣ်.

In a Karen sentence, therefore—

(1) An adjective modifier follows the noun which it modifies.

(2) An adverbial modifier stands after the verb and its object if it have one, but—

(3) An adverbial modifer denoting time may stand at the beginning of the sentence.

PARTS OF SPEECH.

23. The Karen language has the nine following parts of speech: Nouns, Pronouns, Adjectives, Verbs, Adverbs, Prepositions, Conjunctions, Interjections and Particles.

24. But it must be understood that the distinction between the different parts of speech is by no means so sharply preserved in Karen as in English. The same word will appear now as this, and now as that part of speech, according to the office it performs in its sentence. Thus, in the phrase ဟံၣ်အဒိၣ်, *a big house*, ဒိၣ် appears as an adjective; in ဟံၣ်ဒိၣ်ဝဲ, *the house is big*, ဒိၣ် appears as a verb; in ဟံၣ်အတၢ် ဒိၣ်, *the bigness of the house*, ဒိၣ် forms a noun.

COUPLETS.

25. Among the most striking peculiarities of the Karen language are its paired words, or couplets. Where the English would use a single word to express an idea, the

Karen often joins two words to express the one idea, thus forming a couplet. Sometimes two words of analogous signification are united to form a word of slightly different meaning from either; sometimes the couplet consists of two synonomous words, sometimes it consists of a significant root joined to a root which, out of the couplet, has no meaning. Couplets are found among nouns, adjectives, verbs, and adverbs.

NOUNS.

26. Karen Nouns, like those of all other languages, can be divided into Common and Proper Nouns.

27. A proper noun is usually preceded by the name of the class to which the individual belongs; *e. g.*. ကီၢ်ပယီၤ, *Burma*, (ကီၢ် meaning *country*); ဝ့ၢ်တၢကူၣ်, *Rangoon*, (ဝ့ၢ် meaning *city*). Names of men are preceded by the particle စီၤ, *e. g.*, စီၤရှ့ၣ်ယီၣ်, *Saw Shwe Yaw*. Names of women are preceded by the particle နီၢ်, *e. g.*, နီၢ်ဖိဆံး, *Naw Hpo Hsi.*

28. Common nouns may be divided into Primitive Nouns and Derivative Nouns.

29. Primitive nouns are roots which are nouns by virtue of their intrinsic signification. *e. g*, ဟံၣ်, *a house*, လံာ်, *a book*, ထူ, *gold*, ကျိၢ်, *an ox*.

30. Derivative nouns are such as are derived from—

(1) Verbal roots,

(2) Adjectival roots,

(3) Other noun roots

31. Nouns are formed from verbal roots in the following ways—

(1) Abstract nouns of action are formed—

(*a*) By prefixing the particle တၢ် to the verbal root: *e. g.* from the root လဲၤ *to go*, is formed the noun တ

(*b*) By simply using the verbal root as a noun, qualifying it by a demonstrative adjective; *e. g.*, ထို တရားဉ်, *to go.*

(2) Nouns of agency are formed by prefixing ယ, *person*, to the verb, and at the same time affixing ၆; *e. g.*, ယထို တရ၆, *a traveller.* Sometimes the affix ၆ is omitted.

(3) Instrumental nouns are formed by prefixing ၎င် to the verbal root, *e. g.*, ဝ၁, *to paddle*, ၎င်ဝ၁, *a paddle.*

(4) Nouns denoting the *place where an action is performed* are formed by prefixing ၎ာ၁, *place*, to the verbal root; *e. g.*, ဝ, *to sleep*, ၎ာ၁ဝ, *a bed.*

32. Nouns are formed from adjectival roots in the following ways—

(1) Abstract nouns of quality are formed by prefixing တ၁ to the adjectival root; *e. g.*, ၁၁, *good*, တ၁၁၁, *goodness.*

(2) Nouns denoting persons are formed by prefixing to the adjectival root the particle ဝ, which is a contraction of ယ; *e. g.*, ၆၆, *great*, ဝ၆၆, *a ruler*, literally *a great man.*

33. Nouns are formed from other noun roots in the following ways—

(1) Diminutives are formed by adding ၆, *young, little*, to the noun root; *e. g.*, ခွ၆၆, *a dog*, ခွ၆၆၆, *a little dog, a puppy.*

(2) Gentile nouns, and all nouns expressing residence, are formed by affixing ၆ to the name of the place; *e. g.*, ၁၆, *city*, ၁၆၆၆, *citizens.* The particle ယ is generally prefixed as well; *e. g.*, ဗမာ, *Burma*, ယဗမာ၆, *Burmans.*

(3) Two or more noun roots may be combined: *e. g.*, ထကျ၆, *river*, ၆၆ခွ၆၆၆, *knee.*

34. Noun couplets are formed by the combination of two noun roots, each of which is generally followed or preceded by a particle, which serves to connect them; *e. g.*, ၆၆ဆိတ၆၆ယ, or ၆၆ဆိတ၆၆၆, *birds*, တ၁ကျုးတ၁၆၆၆, *grace*, တ၁၁၁ တ၁၁ဝါ, *goodness.* ယထယ၎၁ *my country*, ၆ဗ၁ထို *your de-*

scendents, သ ဟ ၟ အ ဎ, *his buildings.*   In the last three examples the connecting particle is a personal pronoun in the
possessive case.

GENDER.

35. The Karen language recognizes only natural gender,
not grammatical gender.

36.   Nouns denoting objects without life are neuter.
Abstract nouns may also be considered as neuter.

37 A few nouns, mostly expressive of human relation-
ship, are masculine or feminine by their signification; *e. g.*,
ဎ ၟ, *father*, ၈ ၟ, *mother*, ဝ, *husband*, ဠ, *wife*, ၈ၟၛ, *man*,
၈ၟၕၕ, *woman.*

38. The great body of names of living creatures are of
common gender; *e. g.*, ၈သ ၕ, *child*, ဃ ၚ ၕ, *horse.*

39. The gender of such indeterminate nouns may be distinguished by the following affixes—

၈ၟၛ, or ၛ, masculine, applied to human beings.

၈ၟၕၕ, or ၕ ၕ, feminine, applied to human beings.

ဠ, masculine, applied to animals.

၈ၟ, feminine, applied to animals.

E. g., ၈သ ၕ, *child*, ၈သ ၕ ၈ၟၛ, *boy*, ၈သ ၕ ၈ၟၕၕ, *girl*, ဃ ၚ ၕ,
horse, ဃ ၚ ၕ ဠ, *stallion*, ဃ ၚ ၕ ၈ၟ, *mare.*

NUMBER.

40. Karen nouns convey of themselves no idea of number;
e. g., the noun ဟ ၕ may mean *house* or *houses.* The number
is often left to be inferred from the context. When, however, it is desired definitely to mark the number, this can be
done.

41. The singular is denoted by the numeral ဎ, *one*; *e. g.*,
ဟ ၕ ဎ ၕ ᵃ *a house*

42. The plural may be denoted in the following ways—

(1) By the use of a numeral adjective; *e. g.*, ဟံၣ်ခံဖျၢၣ်, *two houses*, ဟံၣ်အၢၣ်ဖျၢၣ်, *many houses*.

(2) By any one of the following affixes—

တဖၣ်, the usual affix; *e. g.*, ဟံၣ်တဖၣ်, *houses*.

သ့ၣ်, used with the vocative, or with pronouns; *e. g.*, ဒီပုၢ်ဝဲၢ်သ့ၣ်ဧၢ, *brethren*, အဝဲသ့ၣ်, *they*.

သ့ၣ်တဖၣ်, used principally with pronouns; *e. g.*, အဝဲသ့ၣ် တဖၣ်, *they*.

တဖု, တဖၣ်ဖု, and သ့ၣ်တဖၣ်ဖု, used occasionally.

(3) The plural, when used to convey the idea of generality, is often expressed by a couplet; *e. g.*, ဟံၣ်ဃီၤဘိၤ. *houses* or *buildings* in general.

(4) တက့ၢ်သ့ၣ် may be used at the end of a sentence which has a plural subject; *e. g.*, ဒီးဝဲဒဲဆူ ကိၢ်ကိၣ်ရှ့ၣ်အပူၤတက့ၢ်သ့ၣ်လီၤ, *And they came into the land of Goshen*.

CASE.

43. Five case constructions may be recognized: Nominative, Possessive, Objective, Vocative and Absolute. The first three correspond to those of the same name in English, and the vocative is the case of direct address.

44. What is here called the absolute case is peculiar to Karen. Its function is to name prominently at the beginning of the sentence, and thus to emphasize, the person or thing about which some statement is made in the remainder of the sentence.

45. In Karen, as in English, the case of the noun is indicated, not by inflection, but by the position of the word in the sentence. Where this is not sufficient, recourse is had to particles.

46. Regularly, the subject precedes the verb, and the object follows it; *e. g.*, ဒီၣ်ဝါသ့ၣ်ဆီၣ်ဟံၣ်လီၤ. *Saw Wa builds*

a house. ၀ိၢ်ဒၢ, the subject, precedes the verb, သူၣ်ထီၣ်, and ဟံၣ်, the object, follows it.

47. Karen nouns, like English nouns, are often governed by prepositions: *e. g.,* ယလဲၤဆူ၀့ၢ်တကူၣ်, *I go to Rangoon.* Here ၀့ၢ်တကူၣ် is governed by the preposition ဆူ. Nouns follow the prepositions by which they are governed.

48. Where in English a verb has two objects, or one direct and one indirect object, the Karen may place either one as the direct object of the verb, and the other will then be governed by the preposition လၢ; *e. g.,* where the English says, *I give Saw Wa a book,* the Karen may say. ယတ့ၣ်စီၤ ၀ါလၢလံာ်တဘ့ၣ်, or ယဟ့ၣ်လံာ်တဘ့ၣ်လၢစီၤ၀ါလီၤ.

49. In Karen, verbal nouns as well as verbs may take objects, *e. g.,* တၢ်အဲၣ်နၤ, *love (for) you.*

50. A noun in the possessive construction is joined to the name of the thing possessed by the particle အ; *e. g.,* ၀ိၢ်ဒၢ အဟံၣ်, *Saw Wa's house.*

51. A noun in the vocative case is followed by the particle ဧၢ; *e. g.,* ၀ိၢ်ဒၢဧၢ, *Saw Wa.*

52. Substantives in the absolute construction stand first in the sentence, free of all grammatical relation thereto. and are usually followed by the demonstrative adjective နၤ or နၣ်, *e. g.,* ဟံၣ်အၣန်ၣ်, ၀ိၢ်ဒၢသူၣ်ထီၣ်အီၤလီၤ, *That house, Saw Wa built it.* Here ဟံၣ် is in the absolute construction. followed by နၣ်, *that.* Occasionally the particle ဧၢ takes the place of the particle နၤ or နၣ်. More commonly it follows one of them; *e. g.,* ဟံၣ်အၣန်ၣ်ဧၢ, ၀ိၢ်ဒၢသူၣ်ထီၣ်အီၤလီၤ.

PRONOUNS.

53. Karen Pronouns are principally Personal, though Interrogative and Indefinite Pronouns exist.

54. There are no Relative Pronouns in Karen. Relative clauses

which they modify by means of the conjunction လၢ, the
pronouns used being personal pronouns of the third person.

PERSONAL PRONOUNS.

55. In Karen, as in English, the personal pronouns are
declined, the cases being marked by case forms. The following tables exhibit the three personal pronouns in their
various numbers and cases. Gender is not distinguished.

	Singular.	Plural.
First Person.		
Nom.	ယ, ဝ	ပ
Poss.	ယ, ဝ	ပ
Obj.	ယၤ	ပၤ
Second Person.		
Nom.	န	သု
Poss.	န	သု
Obj.	နၤ	သု
Third Person.		
Nom.	အ	အ
Poss.	အ	အ
Obj.	အီၤ	အီၤ

56. The form အ for the nominative case of the pronoun
of the third person is confined to subordinate clauses. In
principal clauses this pronoun appears in the singular as
အဝဲ, အဝဲဒၣ်, or occasionally အတၢ်, and in the plural generally as အဝဲသ္ဉ်.

57. After the verb မ့ၢ်, *to be*, the objective forms of the
personal pronouns are used instead of the nominative
forms ; *e. g.*, မ့ၢ်ယၤလီၤ (not မ့ၢ်ယလီၤ), *It is I.*

2

58. Besides the regular pronouns, the Karen possesses a pronominal affix, ဝဲ. This is affixed to verbs in the third person, particularly in subordinate clauses. It is also affixed to pronouns of all persons in forming compounds. When ဝဲ follows a verb it is never an object, although it often looks like one, but always refers to the subject; *e. g.*, လံာ်တၢ၁ဃ၁ ရၢက္ဲၤ၁ဝဲ၃န္၃, ⸱အၢ၁ဒိၢ၁ဧါ, *The book which the teacher wrote, have you seen it?* Here ဝဲ refers to the subject, ဃၢက္ဲၤ၁, and not to the object, လံာ်. In this construction ဝဲ၃န္၃ is often used like ဝဲ.

59. The simple forms tabulated under §55 form a base from which a number of pronominal forms are built up, by means of the particles ဝဲ and ၁န္၃, the word ၣ၁ဝ၁ှ, *self*, and the demonstrative adjectives, အၣ၁, *this*, and ⸱န္၃, *that*. Such forms are generally self-explanatory. Their cases are indicated like those of nouns. For a complete table of all the possible forms of the personal pronouns, with exemplifications of their use, the reader is referred to Dr. Wade's *Karen Vernacular Grammar*, pp.34-39. The more common forms are noted below.

	Singular.	Plural.
1st pers.	ဃၢဝဲၤန္၃, ယဲၤန္၃	ပဝဲၤန္၃
2nd pers.	⸱နဝဲၤန္၃, ⸱နၤန္၃	သုၢဝဲၤန္၃
3rd pers.	အၢဝဲ, အၢဝဲၤန္၃,	အၢဝဲၤန္၃

60. When used absolutely, the personal pronouns appear in the forms noted under §59. The contracted forms ယဲၤန္၃ and ⸱နၤန္၃ are the ones in common use, the primitive forms ဃၢဝဲၤန္၃ and ⸱နဝဲၤန္၃ being seldom met with in this construction.

61. In the plural forms the plural affix သုၢ may be substituted for the particle ၁န္၃, *e. g.*, ပဝဲသုၢ may be substituted for ပဝဲၤန္၃. To any form so arising the plural affix တၢဝ၁ှ may be added giving such forms as အၢဝဲသုၢတၢဝ၁ှ.

62. The absolute forms of the pronoun (like the absolute forms of the noun) are generally followed by one of the demonstrative adjectives အံၤ and နုၣ်, and sometimes by the particle ဧၢ; e. g., ယၤအၣ်အံၤ, အဝဲသ့ၣ်တဖၣ်နုၣ်, နဲအၣ်ဧၢ.

63. In the absolute forms, အၣ် is often omitted; e. g., ယၤ. ယလဲၤတသ့ဘၣ်, As for me, I cannot go

64. In the first and second persons, the objective form often takes the place of the proper absolute form; e. g., နၤ. နကဘၣ်လဲၤလီၤ. As for you, you will have to go.

65. The use of the absolute form is illustrated in the following sentences: ယၤအၣ်အံၤ,ယလဲၤတသ့ဘၣ်, As for me, I cannot go, အဝဲသ့ၣ်တဖၣ်နုၣ်,အဝံၣ်အံၤၣ်လၢအဝ့ၢ်တကျိၣ်အပူၤအံၤ, As for them, their house is in Rangoon.

INTENSIVE PRONOUNS

66. Intensive forms of the personal pronouns are formed by adding to the possessive case the word ကစၢ်, or ကစၢ်ဒၣ်, self, and the particles အၣ်ဝဲ. They are as follows:

	Singular.	Plural.
1st pers.	ယကစၢ်အၣ်ယၤ	ပကစၢ်အၣ်ပဝဲ
	ယကစၢ်ဒၣ်အၣ်ယၤ	ပကစၢ်ဒၣ်အၣ်ပဝဲ
2nd pers.	နၤကစၢ်အၣ်နဲ	သုကစၢ်အၣ်သုဝဲ
	နကစၢ်ဒၣ်အၣ်နဲ	သုကစၢ်ဒၣ်အၣ်သုဝဲ
3rd pers.	အကစၢ်အၣ်ဝဲ	အကစၢ်အၣ်ဝဲ
	အကစၢ်ဒၣ်အၣ်ဝဲ	အကစၢ်ဒၣ်အၣ်ဝဲ

67. These forms are used in apposition with a substantive, for emphasis; e g., စီဝါအကစၢ်အၣ်ဝဲကလဲၤလီၤ, Saw Wa himself will go, ယကမၤယကစၢ်အၣ်ယၤလီၤ, I will do it myself.

68. The same thing may be indicated by affixing the forms အၣ်ယၤ,အၣ်ပဝဲ, etc. to the verb; e. g., သုကလဲၤအၣ်သုဝဲလီၤ, You will go yourselves.

69. The forms mentioned in § 68, affixed to nouns which follow a substantive in the possessive, convey the same idea as the English word *own*; *e. g.*, ယလံာ်ဒၣ်ဃဲ, *my own book.*

REFLEXIVE PRONOUNS.

70. Reflexive forms of the personal pronouns are formed by affixing to the possessive case the word သး, *self.* They are as follows—

	Singular.	Plural.
1st pers.	ယသး	ပသး
2nd pers.	နသး	သုသး
3rd pers.	အသး	အသး

71. These forms are used as the objects of verbs, when the person affected by the action is the same as the person performing it; *e. g.*, စီၤဝါတိၢ်လီၤအသးလီၤ, *Saw Wa beats himself.* These forms always appear as direct objectives while the intensive forms previously described are generally used in apposition. An intensive pronoun, however, sometimes takes the place of a proper reflexive.

72. The Pronoun သါ may also be classed among the reflexives. It takes the place of the personal pronoun of the third person in indirect discourse, referring to the speaker; *e. g.*, စီၤဝါစံးလၢသါကဟဲလီၤ *Saw Wa says that he (Saw Wa) will come.*

POSSESSIVE PRONOUNS

73. The possessive pronouns *mine, thine*, etc. are formed by affixing ဲ or တၢ် to the possessive forms of the personal pronouns; *e. g.*, အဝဲနၣ်မ့ၢ်ယဲ, အဝဲနၣ်မ့ၢ်ယတၢ်, *That is mine.*

74. ဲ and တၢ် may be similarly used with nouns in the possessive [illegible] ၣ်နၣ်မ့ၢ်စီၤဝါအဲ [illegible] or အဝဲနၣ်မ့ၢ်စီၤဝါအတၢ်လီၤ, [illegible]

DEMONSTRATIVE PRONOUNS.

75. Properly speaking, the Karen language has no demonstrative pronouns. Their place is supplied, however, by combining the demoustrative adjectives, သိၢ, *this*, and နၟၣ်, *that*, with the personal pronoun of the third person: အဝဲသိၢ, *this*, အဝဲနၟၣ်, *that*.

INTERROGATIVE PRONOUNS.

76. The interrogative adjectives described in §§ 101, 102 are used also as interrogative pronouns; *e. g.*, နမၤမနုၤလဲၣ်. *What are you doing?* နထံၣ်မတၤတဂၤဝဲၢ်လဲၣ် *Whom do you see?* လၢလံာ်ခံဘ့ၣ်နၟၣ်နအဲၣ်ဒိးမတၤအဝဲလဲၣ်. *Which of the two books do you wish?*

77. The interrogative possessive pronoun, *whose*, is formed by affixing အဝဲ or အတၢ် to the interrogative pronoun မတၤ: *e. g.*, လံာ်အဝဲအံၤမ့ၢ်မတၤအဝဲလဲၣ်, *Whose is this book?*

INDEFINITE PRONOUNS.

78. တၢ် is used as the subject of impersonal verbs; *e. g.* တၢ်စူၤရၢၢ်ၤ, *It rains.*

79. ပှၤ or တၢ် is often used as an indefinite subject to a verb in the third person singular, when we do not know, or do not wish to express, the subject of the verb; *e. g.*, တၢ် (or ပှၤ) တိၢ်အီၤၢ်ၤ, *Somebody beat him.*

80. ပှၤ is often used indefinitely in the objective case, to express people in general.

81. တၢ် is used as an indefinite object to verbs which require one, but to which no definite object can be assigned: *e. g.*, ယထံၣ်တၢ်ၢ်ၤ, *I see*, literally, *I see things.*

82. မနုၤ and မတၤ are sometimes used as indefinite pronouns: *e. g.*. မတၤတဂၤဝဲၢ်ၢ်ၤ, *A certain person came.*

83. Many of the indefinite adjectives described under § 99 are also used as indefinite pronouns; *e. g.*, နမ့ၢ်ထံၣ်ထိၣ် ဒ့ၣ်ဖိးပှၤန့ၢ်ယၤလၢတဘ့ၣ်တက့ၢ်, *If you see any ducks, buy me one.*

ADJECTIVES.

84 Most of the roots which in English would be regarded as essentially adjectival in their signification, are in Karen considered as verbs. Under this head come all the roots expressive of quality, *e. g.*, the root ဂ့ၤ, expressive of goodness, means, not *good*, but *to be good*. So with many roots expressive of quantity, *e. g.*, ဒိၣ် means, not *great*, but *to be great*. And such words are constantly used as verbs, the verbal meaning being the primitive one.

ADJECTIVES OF QUALITY

85. Adjectives of quality are really adjective (relative) clauses in an abbreviated form. "A good man" would originally be expressed by ပှၤလၢအဂ့ၤ, *a man that is good*. But it is commonly expressed in an abbreviated form, ပှၤအဂ့ၤ, the relative conjunction, လၢ, being omitted. It is sometimes still further abbreviated by omitting the pronoun အ, when it would stand simply ပှၤဂ့ၤ.

ADJECTIVES OF QUANTITY

86 Adjectives of quantity in mass are largely expressed by abbreviated relative clauses, like adjectives of quality; *e. g.*, ဟံၣ်အဒိၣ်, *a great house.*

87. Some adjectives expressive of magnitude are formed by prefixing the particle ဖး to verbal roots. Such adjectives [illegible] modify, *e. g.*, [illegible]

NUMERAL ADJECTIVES.

88. The following table shows the cardinal numerals.

1	၁	တၢ်
2	၂	ခံ
3	၃	သၢ
4	၄	လွံၢ်
5	၅	ယဲၢ်
6	၆	ဃု
7	၇	နွံ
8	၈	ဃိး
9	၉	ခွံ
10	၁၀	တဆံ
11	၁၁	တဆံတၢ
19	၁၉	တဆံခွံ
20	၂၀	ခံဆံ
90	၉၀	ခွံဆံ
100	၁၀၀	တကယၤ
200	၂၀၀	ခံကယၤ
1,000	၁၀၀၀	တကထိ
10,000	၁၀၀၀၀	တကလး
100,000	၁၀၀၀၀၀	တကဃၤ
1,000,000	၁၀၀၀၀၀၁	တကကွဲၢ်
10,000,000	၁၀၀၀၀၀၀၀	ထကဘိ

E. g, 13,297,652 would be written ၁၃၂၉၇၆၅၂ and read
ဘကဘိသၢကကွဲၢ်ခံကဃၤခွံကလးနွံကထိဃုကယၤယဲၢ်ဆံခံ.

89. A numeral adjective almost invariably follows the noun which it modifies, and is itself followed by an auxiliary word expressing some quality of the noun to which it refers; *e. g.*, ပှၤခံဂၤ, *two men,* ဂၤ is a numeral affix used in speaking of rational beings. ထွံၣ်လွံၢ်ဒု, *four dogs* ဒု is a numeral affix used in speaking of quadrupeds.

90. The following table, adapted from a similar one in Mason's Karen grammar, gives a list of numeral affixes with a statement of their uses, and examples.

ကတြၢ်, applied to things in bundles; e. g., လံၥ်တကတြၢ်, a book.

ကထၢ, applied to things conceived of as existing in a successive series ; e. g., ယၥ်ခံကထၢ, two blankets.

ကဘျး, applied to things conceived of as existing in thin laminae ; e. g., စးခိခံကဘျး, two sheets of paper.

ကရၢ, applied to companies of persons or animals ; e. g , တၢ်အိၣ်ဖှိၣ်တကရၢ, a church

ကဒၢ, applied to plots of ground ; e. g., စံၥ်တကဒၢ, a field

ကၢ်ၣ်, applied to logs, felled trees etc , e. g., သ့ၣ်တကၢ်ၣ်, a log of wood.

ဒၢ, applied to traps and snares ; e. g., ထၢ့ဒၢ, a trap.

ဒ့ၣ်, applied to things conceived as proceeding from one head ; e. g. ဝၣ်တဒ့ၣ်, a bamboo tree.

ဒ့, applied to sides of things ; e. g., ရံဒ့, two hands.

ဂၢ, applied to rational beings ; e. g., ကလူးခံဂၢ, two angels ပှၤကညီသၢဂၢ, three men.

ခၢ, applied to vehicles , e. g., လ္ၣ်ခံခၢ, two carts.

ဖျၣ်, applied to the eyes, and to large seeds ; e. g., ပနၢ်ၢ် ချံခံဖျၣ်, two jackfruit seeds.

ဖၢ, applied to things occurring at intervals ; e. g., လံၥ် စီဆှံတဖၢ, a chapter of the Bible.

ထံး, applied to trees ; e. g., သဝ်းသ့ၣ်သၢထံး, three mango trees.

ထံၣ်, applied to words or sentences, e. g., တၢ်ကတိၤတထံၣ်, a word, a saying.

ထ့ၣ်, applied to trees, posts, etc., e. g., သ့ၣ်ပဟံၣ်သၢထ့ၣ်, three teak posts.

ဒၢ, applied to bird's nests, e g အိၣ်အသွံၣ်ခံဒၢ, two bird's nests.

ဒ့, applied to quadrupeds; *e. g.*, ကသ့ၣ်ခံဒ့, *two horses.*

ဘ့, applied to bamboos and small trees; *e. g.*, ဝၣ်တဘ့, *one bamboo.*

ဒိ, applied to leaves of the palm and plantain families; *e. g.*, သကွံလၣ်တဒိ, *a plantain leaf.*

ပူၤ, applied to places; *e. g.*, အလီၢ်တပူၤ, *a place.*

ဒိး or ဒိး, applied to flowers; *e. g.*, ဖီတၢ်ဆူၣ်ခံဒိး, *two roses.*

ပု applied to large bodies of men and animals; *e g.*, သိခံပု, *two flocks of sheep.*

ဖ့, applied to felled trees; *e. g.*, သ့ၣ်ပဟံၣ်တဖ့, *a teak log.*

ဖျၢၣ်, applied to things conceived of as spherical; *e. g.*, သဓိးသၣ်လွံၢ်ဖျၢၣ်, *two mangoes.*

ဖျိ, applied to openings; *e. g.*, ဝဲတြီခံဖျိ, *two doors.*

ဘ့ၣ်, applied to things conceived of as flat; *e. g.*, ဆီတဘ့ၣ်, *a foul.*

ဘိ, applied to things conceived of as cylindrical; *e. g.*, ဂုၢ်သၢဘိ, *three snakes.*

ဘီ, applied to blows, words and sentences, *e. g.*, တၢ်ကတိၤတဘီခံဘီ, *a word or two.*

မံၤ, applied to things referred to in an indefinite manner; *e. g.*, တၢ်ခံမံၤသၢမံၤ, *two or three things.*

ယ့ၢ်, applied to songs and poems: *e. g.*, တၢ်သးဝံၣ်ခံယ့ၢ်, *two songs.*

လီၢ် applied to places; *e. g.*, စံၣ်တလီၢ်, *a field.*

91. There are a number of words denoting portions, quantities or collections, which are used in a similar manner to the numeral auxiliaries; *e. g.*, ထံတကွံး, *a drink of water*, ဂ့ၢ်ခံကဒိၣ်, *two bunches of rattans*, ကပံၣ်တဖဲ, *a handful of mud.*

92. When there is no numeral affix proper to a noun, and sometimes even when there is a numeral affix which might be used, the noun itself is repeated after the numeral,

e. g., ဘိမ့်ၢတဘိမ့်ၢ, *a kingdom* ကိၢတဘ္၃်, or ကိၢတကိၢ, *a country*

93. Sometimes there is a choice of numeral affixes for the same noun, *e. g.,* မဲာ်တဘ္၃်, or မဲာ်ထၣ့်, *an eye.*

94. Numerals are sometimes prefixed to the nouns which they modify; *e g.,* တဟံၣ်အ၃်တဟံၣ်, *from house to house,* ခံသၢသၢ, *two or three days.*

95. The numeral affixes regularly follow the numerals with which they stand   But when the numeral is ten or a multiple of ten, the affix precedes the numeral, and is itself preceded by the particle အ; *e. g.,* ဂီၤ်အရခံဆံ, *twenty cattle.*

96. The formation of the ordinal numerals will easily be understood from the following examples—

အဒိၣ်တဲးတဝၢ,	*first (man)*; အဒိၣ်ထံး means *beginning*.
အဒိၣ်ထံးတဝါ.	*first (thing)*.
ခံၢတဝၢ,	*second (man)*
သၢဖၢတဖၢ,	*third (thing)*
လွံၢ်ရတၢ.	*fourth (quadruped)*

97. The ordinal adjectives အဆိကတၢၢ, *first*, and အခံကတၢၢ, *last* are exceptional in their formation. See § 112.

98 Multiplicatives are formed by affixing ဝး to the cardinal numerals. *e. g*, ခံဝး. *twofold*

INDEFINITE ADJECTIVES.

99. The numeral affixes form the basis of a number of common idioms expressing ideas of number or quantity.

(1) Certain indefinite numeral adjectives are combined with the numeral auxiliaries, in the same manner as the cardinal numerals. These are အါ, *many,* ဇၢ, *few,* and တဘ္ျၢ, ……   ……   …… ……   …… တၢကတိၢရၢတၢ, *few words*

(2) The numeral သ, *one*, with an appropriate numeral affix, often has the sense of the English indefinite article; *e. g.*, ဟံ့ဉ်တချ႑ဉ်, *a house.*

(3) The numeral သ, *one*, with a reduplicated numeral affix is used in referring indefinitely to one person or thing; *e. g.*, ပ႑တဝ႑ဝ႑, *some man*, တဆိတ႑ရ႑, *some elephant.*

(4) The indefinite adjective of quantity, တနှိ႑, *some*, is formed from the numeral သ by means of the particle နှိ႑.

(5) The reduplicated form တနှိ႑နှိ႑, is used in referring indefinitely to more than one person or thing; ပ႑တနှိ႑နှိ႑, *some men*, လံဉ်တနှိ႑နှိ႑, *some books.*

(6) In a similar way are formed တစဲ႑. တစဲးစဲ႑. *a little*, တစဲးၫ္ဒၫ္ and တပ္ၫၫ္ဒၫ္, *a great deal.*

(7) Universality is expressed by placing a numeral auxiliary between သ and လၫ္လၫ္. *e. g.*, ပ႑တဝ႑လၫ္လၫ္. *every man.*

(8) The same idea is expressed by placing a numeral auxiliary between ကီး and ဲး : *e g.*, ထိဉ်ကီးဘ့ဉ်ဲး *every bird.*

(9) Completeness is expressed by placing a numeral affix between ၒ and ၫ္ဒၫ္ ; *e g.*, ဟီဉ်ခိဉ်ၒဘ့ဉ်ၫ္ဒၫ္. *the whole earth.*

(10) A complete number may be expressed by affixing ခီဉ်, လ႑ဉ် or ၫ္ဒၫ္ to any one of the ordinal numerals: *e. g.*, သ႑ဝ႑ခီဉ်, သ႑ဝ႑လ႑ဉ်, သ႑ဝ႑ၫ္ဒၫ္, *all three (men).*

(11) Singularity is expressed by placing the numeral သ with a suitable affix between ခဲ and ၒ႑: *e. g.* ခဲတဝ႑ၒ႑. *only one (man).*

(12) Identity is expressed by placing the numeral affix between သ and ၒ ; *e. g.*, ဟံ့ဉ်တချ႑ဉ်ၒ, the same house.

(13) Utter non-existence of a thing is expressed by affixing a numeral auxiliary to နှိသ : *e g.*. လံဉ်တအိဉ်နှိတ႑ဘ့ဉ် သဉ်, *There is not a single book.*

100. Certain other indefinite adjectives of quantity are formed independently of the numeral system. Such are—
ခလၢၣ်, ခလၢၣ်ခဲဆ. *all*, which follows its noun ; *e. g.*, ပှၤခလၢၣ်, *all men.*

ထီရိၤ, *every*, which generally precedes its noun. The noun may be followed by the number one, and this may in turn be followed by လၢ်လၢ် ; *c. g.*, ထီရိၤပှၤ. ထီရိၤပှၤတၢ ထီရိၤပှၤတၢဝၢလၢ်လၢ်, *every man.*

ဒၣၣ်, *whoever*, or *whatever*, which precedes its noun *e. g.*, ဒၣၣ်ပှၤ, *whatever man.*

INTEROGATIVE ADJECTIVES.

101. The common interrogative adjectives are မတၤ, referring to persons, and မနုၤ, referring to things, *e. g.*, နမဲ့ဒီးသရၣ်မတၤလဲၣ်, *With what teacher did you come?* နအဲၣ် ဒီးအီၣ်တၢသၣ်မနုၤလဲၣ်, *What fruit do you wish to eat?* မတၤ and မနုၤ are often followed by တဂၤ and တမံၤ respectively. *e. g.*, သရၣ်မတၤတဂၤလဲၣ်.

102. An interrogative adjective with a selective force is formed by prefixing ဒၣလဲၣ် to the ordinal numeral တ, *one*. which is in its turn followed by the appropriate numeral affix, *c. g.*, နအဲၣ်ဒီးလံာ်ဖဲလဲၣ်တဘ့ၣ်လဲၣ်, *Which book do you wish?*

103 Interrogative adjectives of quantity are made by prefixing ဆံး to indefinite adjectives of quantity; *e g*, ဆံးဒိၣ်, *how great,* ဆံးအၢ, *how much, how many,* နစ္အိၣ်ဆံးအၢလဲၣ်, *How much money have you?* These are used both in direct and indirect discourse. In indirect discourse they sometimes suffer reduplication *g.*, ယစ္အိၣ်ဆံးအၢဆံးအၢလဲၣ် နၣ်ယတသ့ၣ်ညါဘၣ်, *I do not know how much money I have.*

104 Interrogative adjectives of number may be formed by prefixing ဒွိ or ဒွိ to the numeral affix ; *e. g.*, သုကလဲၤ ဒွိဂၤလဲၣ် *How many of you will .?* These also may be used in [...]

DEMONSTRATIVE ADJECTIVES.

105 The Karen language has two definite demonstrative adjectives, အံၤ, အအံၤ, *this*, and နုၣ်, အနုၣ်, *that*. They may modify any substantive element, be it noun, pronoun, phrase or clause.

106. နုၣ်, and occasionally အံၤ, is used to mark the end of a noun clause, or of a series of adjectival modifiers of a noun ; *e g.*, ပှၤသးပှၢ်အဂ့ၤလၢအအိၣ်ဝဲအိးဝဲလၢဝ့ၢ်တကူၣ်အပူၤတဝၢနုၣ်, *The good old man who lives in Rangoon*

107. နုၣ် is often used with the force of a definite article.

108. နုၣ် is commonly used in referring again to something which has just been mentioned.

ADJECTIVAL COUPLETS.

109 Adjectival couplets are affixed to the nouns which they modify. Such a couplet consists of two adjective-verbal roots, each of which is preceded by the particle အ *e. g.*, ပှၤအဂ့ၤအဝါ, *a good man*.

COMPARISON OF ADJECTIVES.

110. The comparative degree is expressed by affixing တက့ၢ် to the adjective ; *e. g.*, ဂ့ၤ, *good*, ဂ့ၤတက့ၢ်, *better*.

111. Where the object of comparison is expressed, the adjective is followed by နၢ် instead of တက့ၢ် ; *e. g.*, ဂ့ၤနၢ်ယၤ, *better than I*. In such cases, the object of comparison is generally followed by တက့ၢ်, *c. g.*, ဂ့ၤနၢ်ယၤတက့ၢ်, *better than I*.

112. The superlative degree is formed by affixing ကတၢၢ် or ကုၣ် to the adjective ; *e. g.*, ဂ့ၤကတၢၢ် or ၍ ၤကုၣ်, *best*.

VERBS.

113. Karen verbs express actions, states or qualities. *e. g.,* လဲၢ, *to go,* အိၣ်, *to be,* ဂ္ၤ, *to be good.*

114. Karen verbs may be divided into transitive and intransitive verbs. Many verbs which in English are regarded as intransitive, in Karen are regarded as transitive, and take an object; *e g .* the verb လဲၢ, *to go,* is often used with the object တၢ်

115. In Karen, a verb which can take an object generally does take one. When no definite object can be assigned, the indefinite object တၢ် is frequently used; *e. g.,* ယထံၣ်တၢ်, *I see.* See §81.

116. Karen verbs have no inflections, properly so called. The accidents of voice, mood, tense, person and number, are expressed by particles connected with the verb, or are left to be inferred from the subject.

VOICE.

117. Three voices may be recognized in Karen, Active, Passive and Middle.

118. The verb in its simple and primitive form is in the active voice, *e. g.,* in the sentence ယထံၣ်နၤလီၤ, *I see you,* ထံၣ် is in the active voice.

119. The formation of the passive voice is peculiar. A few examples will make it clearer than any explanation.

The following sentences exhibit the passive of the verb ထံၣ်, *to see—*

ယဘၣ်တၢ်ထံၣ်ယၤလီၤ,	*I am seen.*
နဘၣ်တၢ်ထံၣ်နၤလီၤ,	*You are seen.*
၀ါဘၣ်တၢ်ထံၣ်အီၤလီၤ	*Saw Wa is seen.*

120. In the last sentence, ၀ါ is the subject, ဘၣ်, *encountered,* the predicate, တၢ်ထံၣ်, *the seeing,* the object of ဘၣ်. ၊ ၊ ၢ ၊ ၊ ၊ ၊ ၊ ၊ ၊ ၊ တၢ်ထံၣ်

121. Occasionally, in the above mentioned form of the passive voice, the reflexive pronouns ယသး, နသး, အသး, etc., take the place of the simple personal pronouns.

122. When it is desired to convey the idea that the subject voluntarily submits to an action, the passive voice is differently expressed. In this case, the verbal root is preceded by 8း or ဂ္ဂ၍ and followed by a reflexive pronoun; e. g , ယ8းထံၩ်ယသး, *I am seen, I permit myself to be seen*; 8ၤဝါဂ္ဂၩ်ထံၩ်အသး, *Saw Wa is seen, submits to being seen.*

123. Closely allied to this second form of the passive voice is a form used to convey the idea that a thing is in a certain state as the result of an action which has been performed upon it; e. g., တၩ်အိၩ်ကွဲးအသး, *It is written.*

124. The middle voice expresses the idea that the subject performs an action upon himself. To express this the active form of the verb is followed by the particle လီၤ, and a reflexive pronoun; e. g., 8ၤဝါ ထံၩ်လီၤအသး, *Saw Wa sees himself.*

MOOD.

125. There are only two moods in Karen, the Indicative and the Imperative.

126. The primitive form of the verb is indicative.

127. The primitive form of the verb may be used in the imperative; e. g., ဃ္ဂ၍, *Run.*

128. When a verb is in the imperative mood the sentence (if expressing a command) commonly ends with the particle တက္ၤ၍; e. g., ဃ္ဂ၍တက္ၤ၍, *Run,* ဟဲဆူယအိၩ်တက္ၤ၍, *Come to me.*

129. The particles လ၍ and ဝ8 are sometimes affixed to the verb in an imperative sentence where the idea is that of entreating a superior; e. g., ဆိၩ်ဂ္ၤဆိၩ်ဝါလၩ်ပှၤတက္ၤ၍, *Bless us.*

130. In giving permission, ကၢိနဲ or ကဒ့ၢ်နဲ sometimes takes the place of တက့ၢ်; *e. g.*, လဲၤကၢိနဲ, *Go.*

131. A sentence expressing a prohibition ends in တဂ့ၤ; *e. g.*, လဲၤတဂ့ၤ, *Do not go.* In such cases the verb may be preceded by သ့ and the negative particle တ, *e. g.*, သ့တလဲၤ တဂ့ၤ, *Do not go.*

132. A precative sentence is introduced by the particle ပ and otherwise has the form of a sentence expressing command or prohibition; *e. g.*, ပပလဲၤတက့ၢ်, *Let us go,* ပပသ့ တလဲၤတဂ့ၤ, *Let us not go.*

TENSE.

133 The verb standing by itself conveys no idea of time. It may refer to past or present time according to the context. *E. g.*, ယလဲၤဝဲၤ may mean *I go, I am going,* or *I went.*

134. An action the performance of which is contemplated, is expressed by prefixing the particle က to the verb. This form is commonly used to express a future action, *e. g.*, ယကလဲၤ, *I shall go, I will go.*

135. The idea of intention or desire is brought out more strongly by prefixing သါ to က, *e. g.*, ဒီၤဝါသါကလဲၤဝဲၤ, *Saw Wa desires to go, intends to go.*

136. Completed action is indicated by affixing the particle လံ to the verb; *e. g.*, ယလဲၤလံ, *I have gone.*

137. The same idea is more emphatically expressed by introducing ဝံၤ before လံ; *e. g.*, ယလဲၤဝံၤလံ.

138 The Karens sometimes use both က and လံ with the same verb to express an intention to perform an action immediately; *e. g.*, ယကလဲၤလံ, *I will go at once.*

139. To mark the completion of an action previous to a certain moment of past time, တ့ၢ် is affixed to the verb, and is [illegible] followed by လံ. [illegible] ယတဘျုးဟဲဝံၤဒဉ်ဒီးအဝဲဒဉ်

ကွၤတူၢ်ဃၣ်, *Before I came he had returned.* This usage is analogous to the English pluperfect.

140. An action dependent upon a supposed condition contrary to fact is sometimes expressed by prefixing တ to the root and affixing တူၢ် or တူၢ်ဃၣ် ; *e. g.,* နခွၢ်တၤဟဲဘၣ်ဒီးယက လဲၤတူၢ်ဃၣ်လီၤ, *If you had not come I should have gone by this time.*

PERSON AND NUMBER.

141. The person and number of the verb are to be inferred from those of the subject : but a verb in the third person sometimes takes ဝဲ after it ; *e. g.,* စီၤပၤဟဲဝဲလီၤ, *The king comes.*

COMPOUND VERBS.

142. Besides the simple verbs, each of which consists as a rule of a single syllable, there are compound verbs formed by combining simple verbs with particles, or with other verbs.

143. A verbal couplet is formed of two verbal roots, each of which is followed by a particle ; *e. g.,* စုၢ်တ္ၤနာ်တ္ၤ, *to believe,* ဒိၣ်ထီၣ်ထိထီၣ်, *to grow up,* ဆံးလီၤဂ္ၤလီၤ, *to decrease,* မၤထီၣ်မၤလီၤ, *to direct,* စီဝဲဆုဝဲ, *to be holy.*

144. The Karen language possesses a number of particles which are combined with simple verbs to make new verbs of kindred signification. Many of these particles were originally verbal roots, and are sometimes used as verbs ; but in the connection under discussion they are to be considered as particles.

145. The following particles are prefixed to the verb—

ထီၣ်, prefixed to a few verbs, has a causative force ; *e. g.,* ထီၣ်ဟူး, *to stir up.*

ဒုး has a permissive or causative force ; *e. g.,* ဒုးလဲၤ, *to dismiss, to send.*

G 3

ပၢ် denotes a representing of the action as if done, often only in appearance; *e. g.*, ပၢ်သံအသး, *to assume the appearance of death.*

ဘိး, prefixed to a few verbs, has a causative force; *e. g.*, ဘိးဘၣ်သ့ၣ်ညါ, *to inform.*

မၤ has a causative force; *e. g.*, မၤသံ, *to kill.*

လီၤ, prefixed to verbs with the negative, indicates that the act is performed imperfectly, or in a slight degree; *e. g.*, ယတလီၤသ့ၣ်ညါဘၣ်, *I scarcely know.*

လီၤ indicates that the subject falls into the state indicated by the verb; *e. g*, လီၤဘုံး, *to become tired.*

လီၤ has also a causative force; *e. g.*, လီၤနံၤ, *to make one laugh.*

ဝံၣ်, prefixed to a few verbs, has a causative force; *e. g.*, ဝံၣ်ဆၢထၢၣ်, *to raise up.*

ဟ့ၣ် has a permissive or causative force; *e. g.*, ဟ့ၣ်အါထီၣ်, *to increase* (transitive).

146. The following particles are affixed to the verb—

ကဒါ has a sense of return, retaliation or opposition; *e. g.*, က့ၤကဒါက့ၤ, *to return.*

ကဒၣ်, or ကဒၣ်ယၢၢ်, has a concessive force; *e. g.*, မ့ၢ်ကဒၣ် ဒ်န့ၣ်လီၤ, *admitting it to be so*, နဝံးတၢ်နၣ်မ့ၢ်ကဒၣ်ယၢၢ်, *admitting the truth of what you say.*

ကဒိး indicates that the same action has been performed before; *e. g.*, သးဝံၣ်ကဒိး, *sing again.*

က့ၤ indicates returning, or repetition of an action, or the performance of an action which there had been a previous unwillingness to perform; *e. g.*, ဟဲက့ၤ, *come back*, နာ်က့ၤ, *believe.*

ကွၢ် indicates that the act is performed by way of trial; *e. g.*, မၤကွၢ် *to try*, လှၣ်ကွၢ် *to taste*.

ကွံၢ် denotes that the action results in a separation; *e. g.*, ပာ်ကွံၢ်, *to put away.*

ဃာ် denotes that the action results in making secure; *e. g.*, စၢဃာ်, *to tie.*

သ့ၣ် denotes that several persons or things act together; *e. g.*, လဲၤသ့ၣ်, *to go together.*

ဆှၢ denotes that the act is done straight forward, literally or figuratively; *e. g.*, ကွၢ်ဆှၢ, *to look off.*

ဒိ indicates that the action is performed from an elevation; *e. g.*, ကွၢ်ဒိ, *to look off* (as from a height).

စၢၤ denotes that the action is performed by way of assistance; *e. g.*, ယကဝၢ်စၢၤနၤ, *I will help you paddle.*

ဆိ denotes that an act is done before some event takes place; *e. g.*, ထံၣ်ဆိ, *to see before.*

တၢ်, affixed to verbs in the negative, indicates that the action is imperfectly or slightly performed; *e. g.*, ယတနာ်တၢ်တၢ်ဘၣ်, *I do not put much faith in it.*

တုၤ denotes that the action results in arriving; *e. g.*, လဲၤတုၤ, *to arrive.*

တ့ၢ် shows that the action is hastened; *e. g.*, လဲၤတ့ၢ်တဲၤတဲၤ, *Come along quickly.*

လီၢ် is affixed to a few words denoting separation; *e. g.*, လီၤလီၢ်, *to fall off.*

ဒၣ် indicates self-originated action; *e. g.*, အဝဲလဲၤဒၣ် အသးၢ်, *He will go of his own accord.* Occasionally it denotes certainty; *e. g.*, တၢ်ကမၤဒၣ်အဝဲအသးဒၣ်နၣ်လီၤ, *It will be sure to happen so.*

ထီ indicates an upward motion; *e. g.*, လဲၤထီ, *to go up.*

ထီၣ် indicates an upward motion, literal or figurative; *e. g.*, လဲၤထီၣ်, *to ascend,* အါထီၣ်, *to increase.* It often denotes incipient action; *e. g.*, အိၣ်ထီၣ်, *to come into being.*

ဒ့ၣ် indicates independent action; *e. g.*, ယကမၤဒ့ၣ်ဃဲာ်, *I will do it myself.*

ဒ့ၣ်ကယါ်, or ဒ့ၣ်ကလိာ်, indicates that the subject defers some other action to perform the one indicated by the verb: *e. g.*, အိၣ်ခိးဒ့ၣ်ကလိာ်, *Wait a bit,* ယကအီၣ်ဒ့ၣ်ကယါ်မ့ၤ, *I will eat rice first.*

နှၤ် indicates that the action results in obtaining; *e. g.*, ထံၣ်နှၤ်, *to find.*

နီၣ် indicates that the action results in observing, *e. g.*, သ့ၣ်နီၣ်, *to remember.*

ပာ်, or ပာ်စၢၤ, indicates that the action is done before some other event; *e. g.*, ဝံးပာ်, ဝံးပာ်စၢၤ, *to promise, to foretell.*

ပၢၤ် indicates that the action reaches unto its object, *e. g.*, လဲၤပၢၤ်, *to go unto.*

ဖုး denotes that the act was done unintentionally, ကိးဖုး, *to utter an involuntary cry.*

ဖျိ indicates that the action results in going through; *e. g.*, လဲၤဖျိ, *to go through.*

ထီး indicates that the action results in an ascent; *e. g.*, ထိၣ်ထီး, *to ascend.*

ဘၣ် indicates that the action passes over onto an object, *e. g.*, ယကတဲဘၣ်အီၤ, *I will tell him.*

ယှၤ denotes that the act is performed by way of assistance; *e. g.*, သးဝံၣ်ယှၤ, *to sing together with one.*

လိ indicates that the act is performed by or for imitation; *e. g.*, သိၣ်လိ, *to teach,* မၤလိ, *to learn.*

လိာ် indicates reciprocal action; *e. g.*, ဒီပုၢ်ဝဲၢ်ကြၢးအဲၣ်လိာ်အသး, *Brothers should love one another.*

လီၤ indicates a downward motion, literal or figurative; *e. g.*, လဲၤလီၤ, *to descend,* စှၤလီၤ, *to decrease.*

သကိး denotes that several persons or things act in company; *e. g.*, ဟဲၤသကိး [illegible]

သကွၢ indicates that the act is performed from a distance; ထံၣ်သကွၢ, *to behold afar off.*

သဒၣ် indicates that the action results in forsaking; *e. g.*, လဲၤသဒၣ်, *to forsake.*

သိ indicates an incipient action; *e. g.*, တၢ်အဝဲဒၣ်ကဲသိစီၤ ပၤန့ၣ်, *when he had just become king.*

ဟ့ၣ် denotes that the action is done carefully or stealthily; *e. g.*, ကွၢ်ဟ့ၣ်, *to watch closely.*

DEPENDENT VERBS.

147. A verb depending on another follows it immediately, without undergoing any change of form; *e. g.*, ယကကျဲး စၢးမၤအီၤလီၤ, *I will try to do it.* This is the common construction for expressing suitibility, necessity, etc.; *e. g.*, အဝဲဒၣ်ကြၢးဟဲလီၤ, *He should come*, ယဘၣ်ဟးလီၤ, *I must go.*

148. Where in English two verbs are connected by the conjunction *and*, in Karen the second verb may immediately follow the first, without a conjunction; *e. g.*, ယကလဲၤ ဃုအီၤလီၤ, *I will go and seek it.*

IDIOMS IN THE USE OF VERBS.

149. The causative verb မၤ and the permissive verb ပျ့ permit the dependent verb to be preceded by a subject; *e. g.*, ပျ့ယလဲၤတက့ၢ်, *Let me go*, အဝဲမၤယလဲၤတ့ၢ်လီၤ, *He caused me to go.* The dependent verb and its subject may be regarded as a substantive clause, forming the object of the causative or permissive verb.

150. Verbs expressing ability stand at the end of the sentence (or clause) preceded by the verb expressing the act in question, with its subject, and object if it have one; *e. g.*, ယဖးလံာ်သ့လီၤ, *I can read.* The verb and its subject may be regarded as a substantive clause forming the subject of the verb of ability.

151. The following list exhibits the common verbs of ability, with their meanings, and examples of their use.

သ္, ability considered with reference to skill, also the generic expression of ability; e. g., ယခဲ့ဖ၊လိတ်၊်တဘ္ူိးယဗး လိ၁သ္လ်ၒ, *I went to school once, and I can read.*

ဂဲ, ability considered with reference to physical health, or inclination; e. g., ယၒိၑ်ဆၟ, ယဟးလိၒဂ့ၜးတဂဲဘ္, *My head aches, I cannot go to walk.*

 နၟ, ability considered with reference to effectiveness of effort; e. g., ဒဲးသမ္ၒၓိၒၒိၗးတၒ်ၒၗ, ယဧၒိၗတနၟဘ္, *The carpenter has work, I cannot hire him.*

ချၞး, ability considered with reference to leisure; e. g., ယဘ္ၒဖ၊လိတၒ်ခဲၒ, ယဟးလိၒဂ့ၜးတချၟးဘ္, *I must study now, I cannot go to walk.*

ဘ္, ability considered with reference to accomplishing the end proposed; e. g., လိၒၒ၁ဝဲၒၖၞ်တလ၊ၒ, ယဗးတၒဘ္ဘ္, *This book is Talaing, I cannot read it.*

ၒၞ, ability considered with reference to the sufficiency of the subject, e. g. တၒ်ဖ၊ၒၞ၊ၑိၒၒၓိၗး ယဖ၊တၒ့၊ဘ္, *The work is too great, I cannot do it.*

152. The ideas of suitability, agreeableness etc., are often expressed in a similar manner to that of potentiality: e. g., နၒၓးကၒသ္ဘ္ၒၖၒ, *Dare you ride a horse?* ယၒ၊ၗးကၒၓ တၑိၒဘ္, *I do not like to ride an elephant,* ဗလဲၒဘ၊ၒတၒ်တၒၒ ဘ္ၒၒ, *Had we not better go to worship?* ယၛၒၒၓိၗကၒသတၒ်ၒ ၾ၊းကၒၓးၒ, *Is it proper for me to buy a silk jacket?*

153 The verb ၒၞ, expressing desire, takes တၒ် for its subject, and is followed by a verb denoting that act the performance of which is desired. This latter verb is followed by သ၊း, *self,* with the possessive case of a pronoun denoting the person who desires to perform the action. Then comes the object of the verb of action generally introduced

to see you, သရၣ်နၣ်တၢ်ဖိၣ်ဖွၢအသးလံာ်တဘ့ၣ်လီၤ, *The teacher wishes to buy a book.*

• **154.** Possession is expressed by the verb အိၣ်, *to be,* in the three following ways—

(1) The possessor stands as the subject, and the thing possessed follows the verb, with which it is connected by the preposition ဒီး, *e. g.,* ယအိၣ်ဒီးလံာ်တဘ့ၣ်, *I have a book.*

(2) Or possessor and thing possessed may change places; *e. g.,* လံာ်တဘ့ၣ်အိၣ်ဒီးယၤ, *I have a book.*

(3) Or the thing possessed, modified by the possessive case of a noun or a pronoun denoting the possessor, may stand as the subject of the verb; *e. g.,* ယလံာ်တဘ့ၣ်အိၣ်ဝဲ, *I have a book.*

ADVERBS.

155. Karen adverbs are mostly derived from other roots, though a few strictly adverbial roots exist.

ADVERBS OF MANNER.

156. Adverbs of manner are regularly formed by duplicating adjective roots; *e. g.,* ချ့ချ့, *swiftly,* ဆူၣ်ဆူၣ်, *strongly.*

157 Adverbs so formed very commonly take the affix ကလဲာ်, *e. g.,* ဆူၣ်ဆူၣ်ကလဲာ်.

158. Sometimes an adjectival root is used in an adverbial sense. This is commonly the case when it is itself modified by another adverb; *e. g.,* စီၤဝါဃ့ၣ်ချ့မး, *Saw Wa runs very fast,* အဝဲဃ့ၣ်တချ့ဘၣ်, *He runs not swiftly.*

159. Some adverbs of manner are formed from verbal roots by means of the affixes ကလၢ, and ကလဲာ်; *e. g.,* အိၣ်ကလၢ, *silently,* ဘိးကလဲာ်, *still.*

160. Occasionally adverbs of manner are formed by prefixing ဂ္ၤ to an adjectival root; *e. g,* ဂ္ၤဂ္ၤ, *well.*

161. Many adverbs of manner are irregular in their formation; *e. g.,* ဘိးကဒီး, * uproly,* ဒီးထံၣ်ခီၣ်ခဲး, *swiftly*

162. Demonstrative adverbs of manner are formed by combining the preposition ဒ်, *like*, with the demonstratives အံၤ and နှၣ်, or with လဲၣ်; *e. g.*, ဒ်အံၤ, ဒ်အံၤအသိး, ဒ်နှၣ်, ဒ်နှၣ်အသိး, *thus*, ဒ်လဲၣ်, *how*, ဒ်အံၤဒ်နှၤ, *somehow*. See § 202.

ADVERBS OF PLACE.

163. Adverbs of place may be formed from the demonstrative adjectives အံၤ and နှၣ် in combination with the prepositions ဖဲ, လၢ and ဆူ. They are exhibited in the following table.

ဖဲအံၤ, *here*, ဖဲနှၣ်, *there*, ဖဲလဲၣ်, *where*, ဖဲအံၤဖဲနှၤ, *here and there.*

လၢအံၤ, *here*, လၢနှၣ်, *there*, လၢလဲၣ်, *where*, *whence*, လၢအံၤ လၢနှၤ, *here and there.*

ဆူအံၤ, *hither*, ဆူနှၣ်, *thither*, ဆူလဲၣ်, *whither*, ဆူအံၤဆူနှၤ, *hither and thither.*

164. The prepositions လၢ and ဆူ form adverbs of place in combination with such roots as ညါ, *front*, ခံ, *back*, ဖး, *above*, လာ်, *below*, ဝၢ်, and ဘး, *beyond*, and ဒိ, *side*; *e. g.*, ဆူညါ, *forward*, လၢခံ, *behind*, လၢဘးဒိ, *beyond*.

ADVERBS OF TIME.

165. Certain adverbs denoting past time are formed by the prefix မ (or မှၢ်) in combination with roots denoting time, as follows—

မကၢဒ်, မကိဒ်, *just now*,
မဆါ, *to-day*,
မဂီၤ, *this morning*,
} with verbs of past time.

မနှၤ, *last night.*
မဟါ, *yesterday.*
မဟါထါ, *the other day.*
မကၢဒ်တဘျီ, မကိဒ်တဘျီ, *last time* (in the immediate past).
[illegible] *l*[illegible] ([illegible])

မဟါတန့်, *last week.*

မါထါတန့်, ,, ,,

• မဟါတလါ, *last month.*

မါထါတလါ, ,, ,,

မငါတ နှၥ်, *last year.*

166. Adverbs expressing future time may be formed in two ways—

(1) By the prefix ခဲ, as follows—

ခဲအီၤ, ခဲကနံၣ်အီၤ, *now,* denoting the immediate future, or the present.

ခဲမဆါ, *to day,*
ခဲမဟါ, *this evening,* } with verbs of future time.
ခဲမုၢ်ၤ, *to night,*

ခဲနီၤ, *to-morrow.*

ခဲတနီၤ, *the day after to-morrow.*

ခဲကီၥ်ၥ်, *in the future.*

ခဲကီၥ်တဘျီ, *next time.*

ခဲကီၥ်တနှ့, *next week.*

ခဲကီၥ်တလါ, *next month.*

ခဲကီၥ်တ နှၣ်, *next year.*

(2) By the use of the prepositions လၢ and ဆူ. Cf. §164. The most common of these are—

လၢခံ, လၢခံကၠၤ, *afterwards.*

ဆူညါ, ဆူညါ5, *in the future.*

ကုၢအံၤဆူညါ, *henceforth.*

167. လၢ is prefixed to some temporal adverbs when the idea of futurity is not implied; *e. g.,* လၢမုၢ်ဆါ5, *by day,* လၢပျၢၤလၢကစၢၤ, *of old.*

168. Another class of temporal adverbs is formed by using temporal nouns like numeral auxiliaries, as follows—

ဆ့တနံၤကၠၤ, *all day.*

သီတၤနံၤကၠၤၤ, *all night.*

သ့သ့တနံၤ. *daily.*

ဘိဘိတနၤ, *nightly.*

ဒိနံၤညါ, *all day*, (similarly ဒိနၤညါ, ဒိနွံညါ, etc)

ကိးမုၢ်နံၤဝဲး, *every day*, (similarly ကိးမုၢ်နၤဝဲး, ကိးနွံဝဲး etc).

169. Many adverbs of time are not formed in accord with any law; *e. g.*, ချ့သဒံး, *quickly*, ထိဘိ, *always.*

170. The roots ဒံး, *still*, *yet*, and လၢၤ, *any more*, are adverbial by virtue of their intrinsic signification. The following examples will illustrate their use: ယဆိကမိၣ်လၢ ယကလဲၤဒံးတဘျုးဘျီလီၤ. *I think I shall still go several times.* အဝဲတဟဲဒံးဘၣ်, *He has not yet come*, ယစ့တအိၣ်လၢၤဘၣ်, *I have no more money.*

NUMERAL ADVERBS.

171. Adverbs denoting *how many times* are formed from the cardinal numerals, in combination with the affix ဘျီ or ရ: *e. g.*, တဘျီ, *once*, ခံဘျီ, *twice*, သၢရ, *thrice.*

172. ဘျီ and ရ are treated like numeral auxiliaries, and may enter into all the combinations of which numeral auxiliaries are capable; *e. g.*, တဘျီဃီ, *simultaneously. at once*, တဘျီဘျီ, တရရ, *sometimes*, ကိးဘျီဝဲး, *every time*, သၢရညါ, *as many as three times.*

173 Adverbs denoting *which time* are formed like ordinal numerals: *e. g.*, အခီၣ်ထံးတဘျီ, *the first time*, ခံဘျီတဘျီ, *the second time.*

174. The particles ရ and ဘျီ enter into certain irregular formations; *e. g.*, ဘျၢနံၤတရ. ဘျၢနံၤတဘျီ, *then.*

ADVERBS OF DEGREE.

175. Some adverbs of degree are formed like the adverbs of manner described in §§ 156 and 157. *e. g.*, ဒိၣ်ဒိၣ်ကလဲာ်, *greatly*

176. The indefinite numeral adjectives described in § 99,
(4), (6), (13), are often used with an adverbial force ; *e. g.*,
ဃတအဲၣ်အိၤနိ့တစဲးဘၣ်, *I do not like it a bit.*

177. The following adverbs are intensive: ဝး, တၢ, နး
(used with adjectives denoting disagreeable sensations),
and ကိၣ် (used with adjectives denoting smallness or
fewness).

178. A moderate degree is expressed by coupling two
contradictory roots, each of which is modified by a negative ; *e. g.* တဒိၣ်တဆံးဘၣ်, တအါတစ့ၤဘၣ်, *moderately.*

179. Other adverbs of degree are irregularly formed;
e. g., လုၤတကူၤ, *not at all* (with negatives), ဃၣ်ဃၣ်, *about*,
ကဲၣ်ဆိး, *too.*

ADVERBS OF COMPARISON.

180. Equality is expressed by ဒ်သိးသိး, *equally*; *e. g.*,
အဝဲဘၣ်နၢ်ပၢၢ်ပံၤယိၤဒီးပှၤကညီဒ်သိးသိးလိၤ, *He understands Burmese and Karen equally*, အဝဲဘၣ်ကတိၤပံၤယိၤဒ်သိးသိးဒီးပှၤကညီ
လိၤ, *He speaks Burmese equally with Karen.*

181. Inequality is expressed by a combination of two
contradictory roots expressive of quantity, *e. g.*, သရၣ်တကြၢး
စံၣ်ညီၣ်ဒိၣ်ဆံးအါရ့ၤပှၤမၤလိတၢ်ဒိဘၣ်, *A teacher should not judge
his pupils unequally.*

INTERROGATIVE ADVERBS

182. Interrogative adverbs of time and place may be
formed from the interrogative particle လဲၣ် ; *e. g.*, ဖဲလဲၣ်,
where, when, လၢလဲၣ်, *where, whence*, ဆူလဲၣ်, *whither.*

183. These are reduplicated in indirect discourse ; *c. g.*,
အဝဲဟဲလၢလဲၣ်လၢလဲၣ်နၣ်ဃၤဝဲတဘၣ်ဘၣ်, *I can not tell whence
he comes.*

184. Interrogative adverbs of quantity are formed by
prefixing ဆံး to adjectives of quantity; *e. g.*. ဆံးအါ, ဆံးဒိၣ်,
how much.

185. These are also repeated in indirect discourse; *e. g.*, ယအဲၣ်အီၤဆံးအၢဆံးအၢလဲၣ်နၣ်ယတဲတသ့ဘၣ်, *I cannot tell how much I like it.*

186. The interrogative adverb of reason is ဘၣ်မနုၤ, *why?* *e. g.*, ဘၣ်မနုၤလၢနတလဲၤယုာ်ဒီးယၤဘၣ်လဲၣ်, *Why do not you go with me?*

ADVERBS OF AFFIRMATION AND NEGATION.

187. Assent is expressed by မ့ၢ် or အၢၣ်.

188. Negation is expressed by prefixing တ to the verb, and affixing ဘၣ်; *e. g.*, အဝဲတဟဲဘၣ်, *He does not come.*

189. A denial is expressed by a negative sentence; *e. g.*, စီၤဝါဟဲဧါ, တဟဲဘၣ်, *Has Saw Wa come?* *No*—literally, *Not come,* တမ့ၢ်ဘၣ်, *No*—literally, *It is not.*

ADVERBS OF PROBABILITY.

190. These are irregular in formation; *e. y.*, ဘၣ်တဘၣ်, သ့ၣ်သ့ၣ်, *perhaps*, သပှၢ်တၢၢ်, *certainly.*

CONJUNCTIVE ADVERBS.

191. The following are conjunctive adverbs of time—

ဖဲ, *when; c. g.*, ဖဲယထံၣ်အီၤနၣ်ယကတဲဘၣ်အီၤလီၤ, *When I see him I will tell him.*

တချုး, *before, e. g.*, ပတချုးလဲၤဒံးဘၣ်ဒီးပကအီၣ်ဒၣ်ကလိၥ်ၦၤလီၤ, *We will eat rice before we go.*

အဖၢမုၢ်, အတီၢ်ၦၤ, *while; e. y.*, အဝဲဒၣ်ဟဲအဖၢမုၢ်ဒီးဘၣ်တၢ်ဆါလီၤ, *He fell sick while he was coming.* See also § 222.

192. ဒ် is used as a correlative conjunctive adverb; *e. g.*, ယဒ်းမၤလိထံၥ်ယဒ်းအဲၣ်ဒီးမၤလိအီၤ, *The more I study, the more I wish to study.*

ADVERBIAL COUPLETS.

193. Adverbial couplets are common; *e. y.*, လၢထံးလၢသီ, *in the beginning* အံၤဒၣ်အံၤနၤ, *here and there*, ကယီၢ်ကယီၢ်, *slowly*

COMPARISON OF ADVERBS.

194. Adverbs which are derived from adjectival roots are susceptible of comparison. An adverb in the comparative or superlative degree is in form exactly the same as the corresponding adjective in the same degree; *e. g.*, ၆ၤဝါဆွၣ်ချၤၣ်အဝဲၢ်တကွၢ်, *Saw Wa runs faster than his brother.*

PREPOSITIONS.

195. The Karen language has seven prepositions, ၆း, ဆူ, လၢ, ၀ဲ, သကူၤ, ၀းတၢ်း, and ၆.

196. ၆း, means *with:* it governs the objective case.

197. ဆူ means *to* or *towards:* it governs the objective case ; but often, instead of governing the noun directly, the aid of a secondary noun is brought in. See §§ 198, 199.

198. လၢ means *at* or *from,* according to the context. It seldom governs a substantive directly, but usually governs a secondary noun, which is modified by the principal substantive, in the possessive case. လၢ in itself is extremely indefinite, and these secondary nouns are brought in to make the meaning more definite.

199. The more common of the secondary nouns are exemplified below—

လၢပ၆၆ၣ်အအိၣ်,	*from the Governor.*
လၢထူၣ်ဝါအ၆ၤထံး,	*by* or *near Htu Wa.*
လၢ၆ၤပၤအ၆ၣ်ထံး,	*at the king's feet.*
လၢယယၢၤ,	*by my side.*
လၢဟံၣ်အမဲၥ်ညါ,	*in front of the house.*
လၢဟံၣ်အဆၢၣ်၆,	*behind the house.*
လၢထူလၤအချၤယဲ,	*behind Tun Hla.*
လၢဟိၣ်၆ိၣ်ချၢ,	*on the earth.*
လၢယ၆ၤ,	*on me*—literally, *on my surface.*
လၢဟံၣ်အပူၢ,	*in the house.*
လၢစပွဲအ၆ိၣ်, လၢစပွဲၣ်ိၣ်,	*on the table.*

လၢအခိၣ်,	*on his head.*
လၢဟံၣ်အဖီလာ်,	*under the house.*
လၢဟံၣ်အကျါ,	*among the houses.*
လၢဟံၣ်အဘၢၣ်စၢႏ,	*between the houses.*
လၢဟံၣ်အဃၢႏဝႏဝႏ,	*round about the house.*
လၢယမါအဂီၢ်,	*for my wife's sake, for my wife.*
လၢတၢ်အံႏအယိ,	*on account of this, because of this.*
လၢကိၢ်ပၤယိၤအဂ့ၢ်,	
လၢကိၢ်ပၤယိၤအဂ့ၢ်အဂီၢ်,	*about Burma.*
လၢကိၢ်ပၤယိၤအဂ့ၢ်အကျိုႏ,	
လၢထံဖီႏခိၣ်,	*on the surface of the water.*

200. ဒ် means *in.* It may govern the objective, or may be used with a secondary noun, like လၢ.

201. သကုၤ, *throughout,* and ဝးတရံႏ, *round about,* govern the objective.

202. ဒ်, *like, as,* always governs the secondary noun အသိႏ, the object of comparison being placed in the possessive case; *e. g.,* အပျဲၢ်မၤဒ်သရၣ်အသိႏနၣ်လီၤ, *The pupil acts like the teacher.* Sometimes the object of comparison is a noun clause, when ဒ် corresponds in meaning to the English *as; e g.,* အပျဲၢ်မၤဒ်သရၣ်မၤဝဲအသိႏနၣ်လီၤ, *The pupil does as the teacher does.* See §§ 211, 228.

CONJUNCTIONS.

203. The Karen language has few conjunctions, supplying their place with phrases which are equivalent to conjunctions. A classified list of the conjunctions, together with the more important conjunctive phrases, will be found below.

COPULATIVE.

204. ဒီႏ, *and,* connects words. phrases or clauses. It may stand at the close of the preceding clause. or at the beginning of the following one.

ဒိး—ဒိး, *both—and;* e. g., ကစၢ်ယွၤတ့ၡဝိၤဒိးမုၢ်ဒိးလါ, *The Lord God created both sun and moon.*

ဒိ—ဒိၢ်, *and also;* e. g., နဲဒိၢ်ဝိၣ်ဒွိ၊, ယဲဒိၢ်ဝိၣ်ဒွိ၊, ပတဖုၢ်ၤဘၣ်, *You are a man and I also am a man, we are not afraid.*

မၤကဒိးတဘၠိ (or တၡ), *again.*

လၢအံၤ (or န္ၣ်) အမဲၣ်ညွ၊, *moreover.*

လၢအံၤ (or ၮၣ်) အဒိဒိၣ်, *moreover.*

အဒိၣ်တၡဒိၣ်, *not only so.*

တမ့ၢ်ထဲ, *not only so.*

ADVERSATIVE.

205. မ့မ့ၢ်, မ့ၢ် (at the beginning of a clause) *but.*

ဘၣ်ဆၣ်, ဘၣ်ဆၣ်ဒိး, *but.*

မ့တမ့ၢ်ဘၣ်ဒိး, *or else.*

သ့ၣ်—သ့ၣ်, *either—or.*

သ့ၣ်သ့ၣ်—သ့ၣ်သ့ၣ်, *either—or.*

ၣ၊—ၣ၊, *either—or.*

ၣ၊ၣ၊—ၣ၊ၣ၊, *either—or.*

မ့ၢ်ၣ၊—မ့ၢ်ၣ၊, *either—or;* e. g., ဆိဒ္ၢ်ၣ၊ထိၣ်ဖ္ဥ်မ့ၢ်ၣ၊ဖ္ၤၮ်ၢ်ယၤ လ၊တၵ္ၣ်တက္ဥ်ၢ်, *Buy me either a foul or a duck.*

ILLATIVE.

206. မိၕၮ္ၣ်ဒိး, မ့ၢ်ၕၮ္ၣ်ဒိး, အၵ္ၢ်မ့ၢ်ၕၮ္ၣ်ဒိး, မ့မ့ၢ်ၕၮ္ၣ်ဒိး, မၤသးၕ ၮ္ၣ်ဒိး, အအံၤဒိး, အၮၣ်ဒိး, and a few other phrases, take the place of the illative conjunction *therefore.*

207. The temporal adverbs တုၤၮ၊ၤတၡ and တုၤၮ၊ၤတဘၠိ, *then,* sometimes have the force of illative conjunctions.

CAUSAL.

208. အၵ္ၢ်ၕအံၤ, အၵ္ၢ်ၕခ်လဲၣ်, မ့ၢ်အၵ္ၢ်ၕခ်လဲၣ်, *because.*

မ့ၢ်မ့ၢ်လၢ, အၵ္ၢ်မ့ၢ်လၢ, *because.*

သတးဒိး, *because.* This stands at the end of its clause; e. g., ယၚၡၤသတးဒိးယပ္ၤၢအိၕဝ္တၤသ္ဘၣ်, *I cannot buy a jacket because my money is scant.*

HYPOTHETICAL.

209. တၢ, *when.*

တၢမ့ၢ်, *if.*

မ့ၢ်, *if.* In this sense မ့ၢ် stands stands immediately after the subject. See § 223.

ဘၣ်ဆၣ်, *though,* stands, in this sense, at the end of the clause it modifies.

နာ်သက့, သနာ်က့, *though,* stands at the end of its clause; *e. g.,* အပှ့ၤဒိၣ်နာ်သက့ (or ဘၣ်ဆၣ်ဒီး) ယကပှ့ၤအီၤလီၤ, *Although the price is high, I shall buy it.*

မ့ၢ်နာ်သက့ဒ်န့ၣ်ဒီး, *nevertheless.*

TELIC.

210. လၢ, *that.* See § 220.
ဒ်သိး, ဒ်သိးဒီး, *in order that.* See § 225, 226.

COMPARATIVE.

211. The preposition ဒ်, governing the secondary noun သိး, performs the function of a comparative conjunction. See §§ 202, 228.

INTERJECTIONS.

212. The Karen language has numerous interjections, for which consult the dictionary.

PARTICLES

213. Most of the particles have been treated under the various parts of speech. A few which cannot be so treated to advantage are described here. They are used at the end of sentences to indicate the character of the sentence.

AFFIRMATIVE PARTICLES.

214. လီၤ is used with simple affirmatives.

သၢၣ် implies that the statement is a matter of course.

ယၢဉ် implies assent or concession.

နဉ်, ကၢ်နဉ်, or ကၣ်နဉ် is generally used in reply to questions.

မးလဲၣ် has an emphatic or exclamatory force.

NEGATIVE PARTICLES.

215. ဘၣ် (colloquially, ဘၢၣ်) is used at the close of a negative sentence.

ဖျဉ်လဲၣ်, ဖြဉ်လဲၣ် imply that the statement is probably not true.

မးလဲၣ် has an emphatic or exclamatory force.

INTERROGATIVE PARTICLES.

216 ဧါ is used after a direct question; *e. g.*, နဒိၣ်ဆူၣ်ဧါ, *Are you well?*

လဲၣ် is used after an indirect question; *e. g.*, နလဲၤဆူလဲၣ်, *Where are you going?* In conversation လီၣ် often takes the place of လဲၣ် It may also enter into any of the combinations into which လဲၣ် enters.

ဧါ—ဧါ are used in an alternative question; *e. g*, နအဲၣ်ဒိး သက္ၢ်သၣ်ဧါ သခီၤသၣ်ဧါ, *Do you want a plantain or a mango?*

ဧါ—လဲၣ် are used in alternative questions, especially in indirect discourse; *e. g.*, အဝဲဟဲလၢပသံၣ်ဧါလၢဟိကတၢးလဲၣ်နၣ် ယတသ့ၣ်ညါဘၣ်, *I do not know whether he comes from Bassein or Henzada.*

ဓဲၣ် is equivalent to ဘၣ်ဧါ.

IMPERATIVE PARTICLES.

217. တက့ၢ် marks a command တဂၤ a prohibition, ကၢ်နဉ်, or ကၣ်နဉ်, a permission or a somewhat [illegible] t.

PRECATIVE PARTICLES.

218. ဒ၌, at the end of a declarative or imperative sentence, asks for consent. Hence it softens a command into a request. *E. g.*, ပကတ္ၤဆူဟံၣ်ဒ၌, *We will go home, shall we not?* မၤစၢၤယၤတက့ၢ်ဒ၌, *Help me, won't you?*

SYNTAX OF SUBORDINATE CLAUSES.

219. Subordinate clauses are not only introduced by a conjunction or some equivalent part of speech, but where they do not stand at the end of the sentence they are also terminated by a conjunction or other particle.

220. Noun clauses may be introduced by လၢ and terminated by နၣ်; *e. g.*,· ယတသ့ၣ်ညါလၢအကမၤဝဲၤနၣ်ဘၣ်, *I do not know that he will do it.*

221. Adjective clauses are introduced by လၢ and terminated by နၣ်; *e. g.*, လံာ်လၢသရၣ်ကွဲးဝဲနၣ်အိၣ်လၢစီၤတဘ္ၣ်ဒိၣ်လိၤ, *The book which the teacher wrote is on the table.*

222. Some adverbial clauses are introduced by လၢ, ဖဲ, or ဖဲၤ, and terminated by a temporal particle, or by နၣ်, *e. g.*, ဖဲၤယထံၣ်ဘၣ်အီၤနၣ်ယကတဲဘၣ်အီၤလိၤ, *When I see him I will tell him.* ယဟံၣ်အိၣ်ဖဲစီၤဝါအဟံၣ်အိၣ်ဝဲၤနၣ်လိၤ, *My house is where Saw Wa's house is,* လၢယဟဲအတိၢ်ပုၤနၣ်ယတထံၣ်ဘၣ်ပုၤနီ တဂၤဘၣ်, *While I was coming I saw nobody.*

223 Conditional clauses are introduced by မ္ၢ်, which stands immediately after the subject, and are terminated by ဒီး; *e. g.*, တၢ်မ္ၢ်စူၤဝဲဒုၤဖိးပကဘၣ်ဒီၣ်လိၤ, *If it rains we shall get wet* An apparent, but not a real, exceptio. to this rule is found in the case of complex sentences, in which a subordinate noun clause will come before မ္ၢ်; *e. g.*, နလၤ မ္ၢ်သ့ဖိ·ဘ္ၤဂၤ၁၆ *If ... ... .ll ... ..*

224. မ့ၢ် is occasionally used to introduce a concessive conditional clause ending in သနာ်က့, or ဘၣ်ဆၣ်; *e. g.*, တၢ်ၡ့ၢ်ဟဲရူၤသနာ်က့ပကဘၣ်လဲၤလီၤ, *Even though it rains we shall have to go.*

225. Clauses of purpose are introduced by ဒ်သိး, or ဒ်သိးဒီး, and when not standing at the end of the sentence are terminated by ဒီး; *e. g.*, ယဟဲဆူကိၣ်ဒ်သိးယကမၤလိလံာ်, *I came to school that I might learn.* ဒ်သိးနကအိၣ်ဆူၣ်ထိၣ်က့ၤဒီးနဘၣ်အီကသံၣ်, *In order that you may recover, you must take medicine.*

226. Negative clauses of purpose take the form of a prohibitory clause preceded by ဒ်သိး, and terminated (when necessary) by ဒီး; *e. g.*. ဒ်သိးနသုတဘၣ်စီၣ်တဂ့ၤဒီးနဘၣ်ဗိၣ်သဒၢမုၢ်, *In order that you may not get wet, you must carry an umbrella.*

227. Negative clauses of purpose are sometimes left without an introductory particle, and are terminated by ဘၣ်ဖုး; *e g.*, အီၣ်အီၤတဂ့ၤ, ထိးအီၤတဂ့ၤ, သုကသံဘၣ်ဖုးလီၤ, *Eat it not neither touch it, lest ye die,* ယခီၣ်ဖံးကဘၣ်စီၣ်ဘၣ်ဖုးဒီးယခီထံ တဘျၢၣ်ဘၣ်, *I dare not cross the river lest my shoes get wet.*

228. Clauses of comparison are introduced by ဒ် and terminated by အသိးန့ၣ်, *e. g.*, ဒ်စီၤဝါမၤဝဲအသိးန့ၣ်, ထူသၣ်မၤဒ်န့ၣ် အသိးစ့ၢ်ကီးလီၤ, *As Saw Wa does, so does Tun Tha also.* See § 202, 211.

CPSIA information can be obtained
at www.ICGtesting.com
Printed in the USA
BVHW04s2356130818
524302BV00010B/42/P